MINI CAB TO BEDLAM

by

Typeset and Published by
The National Poetry Foundation
(Registered Charity No 283032)
27 Mill Road
Fareham
Hants PO16 0TH
(Tel/Fax 01329 822218)

Printed by
Consort Print Services
Consort Court, High Street
Fareham, Hants PO16 7AL
(Tel 01329 822530)

Sponsored by Rosemary Arthur

Cover photograph by the author
Photograph of author by Kippa Matthews

Edited by Johnathon Clifford

Poems previously published in *Candelabrum, Dandelion Arts Magazine, First Time, Pause, Phras 96 Winners' Anthology* and *The Third Half.*

ISBN 1 900726 70 X

CONTENTS

I was halfway across America at the dividing line between the East of my youth and the West of my future, and maybe that's why it happened right there and then, that strange red afternoon

From 'On The Road'. Jack Kerouac 1957

For Virginia Green
and
Tim Lawes

GRAVE

He was a good man, the 689th corpse
They carried up the municipal gravel.
Didn't deserve the disrespectful
Rain that drove in hard grey sheets
Across the sodden burial ground,
And gathered clouds of relatives
In black, or close approximations,
From the back of moth-ball wardrobes.

Behind a hedge, we lent on shovels.
Drank our tea and watched the death-flock
Chain smoke awkward silences,
Before the Vicar's brief recital
Drew a sob of insincere
Condolences for fifty quid;
While those with cynical minds dissected
Wills for some bequeathed possession
Left for love or secret guilt.

Afterwards they milled about,
Until the light was growing thin,
And we were anxious to fill in
This mess of mud and previous bone
Residing in the double plot;
And felt no shame at footprints left
Upon their loved-one's varnished box.

THE REPORTER

What news did you *expect* to find
Amongst these arable parishes
Of serfs and scattered manor houses,
Left out of the Doomsday Book
And wholly insignificant since?

You thought your big-smoke wits could pick
These pockets sewn into The Downs
Of all their juicy tabloid scandal,
Bodies in the choked canal
And priests forgetting chastity;

But found the columns dull as Sunday
Spent in front of *Songs of Praise*,
At this, the writer's Russian front
Of primary school nativities,
And weddings where the bride wore . . .
Nothing; well imagination
May as well run riot when
Confronted by a blank screened Mac.

And dreaming of your Pulitzer prize,
You hoped a passing plane would crash.

ICE CREAM MAN

That nomad of the council estate
Had *Teddy Bears Picnic* amplified,
And MIND THAT CHILD! in painted bubbles
From the mouth of Mr Softee -
Circa nineteen-seventy-five,
When I was there in flares and tank tops
With the other kids on tiptoe
For a fix of additives
And psychedelic vermicelli
From the seemingly bottomless freezer
Chock-a-bloc with squashed choc ices,
Strawberry Mivvis, just the one
Cornetto and a Cider Barrel -
Loads of stuff that never matched
The stickers on the serving hatch,
From which a man with tattooed swallows
Up his neck, squeezed raspberry sauce
As though there were an art to it,
And never told us how you end
Up working in an Ice Cream Van.

BRIEF ENCOUNTER

It could have been a *Brief Encounter*,
If the age of steam had lasted
Past the years of harmless smoking.

Stood beside suburban tracks,
I could have freed your eye from grit
With the corner of a handkerchief,
If trains had not turned dull, electric
Carriers of suited stiffs
All in contempt for my appearance.

Glancing up, you did not see
The eyes that lingered on your legs;
Distracting me from Wuthering Heights,
And thinking you were terribly nice,
In a Noel Coward sort of way.

And as we share this common bond;
Unseen, yet somehow destiny,
To end up at a station buffet
With the trill of Cockney banter
As a side-show to our main
Attraction over tea and scones,
Before the final train announcement.

MUMMY

Behind the fingerprinted glass
Of thermostat-controlled oblivion,
You lay without internal organs.
Nothing more, now time has passed,
Than shrunken leather cavities;
A skull stuffed full of Potpourri
(Or something) that the priests stitched in
With spells and incantations meant
To light the synapse stars collapsed
In heavens of a hook-drawn mind.

On some curator's cluttered shelf
Your brain - a numbered artefact -
Floats blankly in formaldehyde;
Amid a sea of glass-distorted
Faces that revolve like suns
Around your cold eternity.

And though their minds have analysed,
And cut you in their thirst for knowledge,
None can see your journey's end
Or comprehend the silent dreams
That white-kneed thieves once interrupted
From the gin and tonic shade,
With glinting mirror trickery
That lit your buried ante-chamber
With a fly-blown foreign sun;
And let them steal your wrapped remains
For someone else's King and Country.

NORTHERN LINE

This dark and bloodless artery
Is clogged with late appointment keepers,
Craning necks expectantly,
As if their wills combined might pull
An object from the lampless gullet,
Or ignite a tunnel spark
And breath of some unnatural wind
To bring another train *(delayed*
By signal problems at East Finchley)
To their lives - inconsequential
Microbes in this forked intestine.

Underground, the women murmur
Lipstick ringed obscenities.
All tits and tuts as time elapses
Slow as forming stalactites;
The gods of their denominations
Unified in common curse
Against a faceless enemy
That causes spiral-staired descent
With antiquated escalators;
Turning idle gears and pulleys
To the task of winding up
Our dull, collective clockwork mind.

Beneath the haloed station names,
There beats a heart of jackboot black,
With death-head skull's insignia
That utter no apologies
At us who herd the postered bowels
Of London, where the streets are paved
With vomit (well, they are in Camden);
Keeping eyes averted from
The stares of would-be psychopaths
And nutters in the community.

MUNICH BEER GARDEN

They know how to pull a pint in Bavaria.
Tall, one litre foaming glasses
Served in leafy garden shade
With pretzels and the oom-pah-pah
Of music dripping from the trees.

After one, I was enchanted
By the sunlight-dappled scene.
After two, I thought I'd died
And gone to a lager drinker's heaven.
After three, I started singing
Two World Wars and one World Cup
At which point I was asked to leave.

DRIFTWOOD

Driftwood - strewn like sun-bleached bones
From something that the tide dismembered,
Lies beyond the foamy reach
Of fingers that would take it back
To islands of imagination -
If I did not pick it up
To see how seas have cossetted
A smoothness from the once-gnarled limbs
That break with satisfying snaps -
Like backs of salt-white stick insects;
And crackle in a fire tinged
With colour when the sand grains catch
And dance like flame-haired hula girls,
While pelicans hug the windswept shore
In lazy squadrons on a thermal.

VICIOUS CIRCLES

Macari's Caff. A sea front dive
Of chequered, fag-scorched melamine.
Where candidates for cancer coughed
Their guts up over tabloid press,
And ashtray dogs with stubbed-out heads
Went chasing twisted tails of blue
In nineteen sixties decor heaven -
Sun-burst gold but miserable
As sin in out-of-season Bognor Regis.

Days crawled by on hands and knees
Like refugees from better times;
When local rags had *sits vac* pages,
And the pier was barbed wire free.

I used to let the chipped cup circus
Stage its greasy act around me
While I juggled poetry
That someone, somewhere, would reject
With comp slips stamped "not quite our thing,
But re-submit when you are published."

Vicious circles, like the patterns
On the age-discoloured lino.

Now I stick two fingers up
At everyone who doubted me.

WALL STREET

Thirty storeys separate
This balcony from gridlocked streets,
Where yellow cabs and black umbrellas
Travel without visible means
Through rain and man-made mountain ranges
In a choreography
That looks distinctly Busby Berkeley
From this architectural shelf -
Enclosed by railings like a basket
Slung beneath a Zeppelin cloud
That steers a route through lightening rods
And granite angel congregations,
Juxtaposed with heating ducts
Of 20th Century functionality.

How much speed would a flower pot gather
In the grip of gravity?
I pictured terracotta bombs
Exploding in a shower of earth
And petals on the rain-soaked asphalt;
Wondering whether human limbs
Would fall to much the same conclusion -
Sprawled out in a spineless state
Of jellyfish rigidity;
Another sidewalk obstacle
For Wall Street's finest to avoid.

COACH PARTY

A day out for the OAPs,
From Lewisham to Camber Sands -
With sandwiches in *Sunblest* bags,
And tartan flasks of lukewarm tea.
It's amazing what you see
As towns and fields blur past at speed.
"Look Bert, there's the Taj Mahal!"
(Takeaway, not mausoleum),
And one of them new thingamajigs
That were not here before the war
When we went hopping down in Kent.

But Camber Sands is just the same;
And if we won the lottery
We'd buy a little bungalow
To overlook the sculptured beach
That internets and cyber space
Will take at least ten years to reach -
And ruin, if it means the loss
Of strawberry knickerbocker glories
And a few striped deckchairs scattered
Like the bodies at Dunkirk;
"These young folk have so much to learn."

And then it's back to Lewisham,
To block the roads with Mini Metros.

AGENT ORANGE

The US Government retired me.
Left me on this military base,
Collecting dust beneath tarpaulin.

It's not so long since I was Agent
Orange, behind enemy lines
To do the President's dirty work
And flush out unseen enemies
For G. I.'s whistling *Purple Haze*
And smoking dope while children burned -
I never could discriminate
What lay beneath that foliage.

Sometimes it was US troops,
And then the Suits would have to blame
The Gooks until it all blew over.

All I did was follow orders;
Tried to keep democracy
By hectares of deforestation.
Then when we had fled Saigon,
The nation was ashamed of me.
Said I was bad for public relations;
Swore they'd never let me out.
Left me on this military base
Collecting dust beneath tarpaulin.

COUNCILLORS

They come, these pious hypocrites,
In gloves and formal overcoats
To church each Sunday, so that others
Of their kind may note their presence
On the pews that backsides polish
Purely for appearances.

In silent contemplation on
The current mortgage interest rates,
They sit throughout the psalms and sermons,
Careful to ignore the bit
That mentions camel, eye and needle -
Surely their attendance record
Counts for something when confronted
By St. Peter at the gates

Assuming he ignores the bribes,
Corruption and discreet back-handers
Taken from the building firms
For passing planning applications;
And the Twin-Town trips abroad
With alcohol and tarts on tap -
All paid for through our council tax,
And now the subject of enquiry.

No-one would suspect a man
Who has the vicar round for tea.

MOULES MARINIERE

Colours deepen from the natural
Purple-black to japalac,
In wine and sliced translucent onion -
Simmered in the pan until
The stubborn shells are prised apart
Like four-and-twenty blackbirds singing
Open-beaked by candlelight;
Or embryonic aliens
Torn limb from limb inside their craft.

The tool we use to wrestle free
These occupants is primitive.
A still-jointed shell without its mollusc,
Wielded like a fairground grab -
Supposed, I think, to make us feel
Like chunky-jumpered fishing folk,
Or rustic, with our hunks of bread
Beyond white linen luxury,
And paying ninety francs a head.

CUBAN SANDWICH SHOP

Nothing disturbs the dead of noon,
In state with sun-dried window flies
And backward letters, casting shadows
On the gold-faced polygons
That seep across the scrubbed wood counter,
Over knives and cold meat haunches,
To a row of gargoyles perched
On leatherette stools; their thoughts like shipwrecks
All adrift on caffeine seas.

At certain times of the afternoon
Shafts of sunlight conjure ghosts
That chew on fat cigars and sway
With dust-motes in slow motion sambas
To the rhythm of the clock;
Its tick a tired requiem
For all the closed tobacco factories
In a town consumed by weeds

That grow unchecked in vacant lots,
And profit from the apathy
Of stubbled welfare cheque dependants
Slouched beneath the sun-bleached awnings
Of a Cuban Sandwich Shop;
Their dreams as caged as glass-domed doughnuts
In the brick and sidewalk swelter.

VIEW FROM A TRAIN

The rooftops' naked clarity
Forms symmetries of backbone grey;
Like shingle-scaled snakes that wait
For sun to warm their terracotta
Pots in lines of stark erections -
Stiff against the smokeless dawn;
And windows yawning fume-dark panes
At pigeons puffed up on the sill.

This time of morning, only milkmen
Clink the still deserted streets;
Their slow electric hum a mantra
To the wires of stuka starlings
Taking turns to straffe the night-swept
Rows of sleeping terraces
That blink their bleary curtained eyes
At puddles making silent movies
Of each keystone cumulus.

WEDDING DAY

We stood there in the pink suede album;
Blessed by sun - our great grins beaming
Out towards a new beginning.

Had you opted for the money,
It would not have been me there
Beside you in the hired clothes;
A dolt transformed into a husband
By the rings with which we wed.

For worse, for poorer, vows have made you
Bound by God to be these things
Forever (or until the cupboard
Cannot keep the skeletons
From spilling all my sordid beans).

Each picture has you innocent,
But one day will our crockery
Be thrown and smashed to smithereens?
Or will we fight for custody
Of those bone china figurines
Your deaf Aunt Edna brought from Wales?

None could see what lay beyond
That bright but windswept afternoon;
Except perhaps the weathercock,
Who sees us born, then wed, then dead.
From high up on the village steeple
He could see confetti strewn
Across our brambled path to nowhere.

UGLY BABY

Nobody wants to say it.
The great unspoken truth that seems
As bad as saying “fuck” in church -
“My god, your baby’s ugly.”

I’m daring you to do it -
Wait until the Loch Ness head
Of Nephew, Niece, or second cousin
Looms up like a fat full moon,
Then tell your beaming relatives
Their offspring has lopsided ears
And eyes that seem to penetrate
Your soul with their unearthly stare.

But no-one does - well, not in public.
Maybe it’s because they harbour
Fears their own child will be uglier.

TWENTY FIVE

Twenty five. A gull-pierced whiteness
Seen from quays afloat on mist.
This was not the future waiting
Out beyond saluted freckles,
Squinting at a brighter sun
With burnt corneas. Gulls went wheeling
In a sky that seemed so wide
With promise that I almost was
Blacked out between canvasses
On Lambrusco afternoons,
Or painting nudes reclined in violets
On some hill in Tuscany.
But now the sky coagulates
With darkling patterns, fraught
By bitterness; the age of disillusion come
To permeate my worthless art.

DEAD MEAT

A carcass is hung
In the wild West End,
In a gallery full
Of some fools who believe
In the Emperor's new clothes
And an Artist Messiah -
Revered for the way
That he turned the flesh green.
They nodded and sniffed
At the high Summer stench,
Pretended to know
What the Artist had meant
By flies that they thought
Were a part of the scene -
Buzzing in typhoid-delirious dream,
While critics went spilling
Their red wine pretensions;
Fawning like lackeys
In front of the Queen.
But nobody cared
That the price was immense,
For *this* was nineties innovation;
Pushing the boundaries of contemporary art
To broad and brilliant new horizons,
With the clever
Juxtaposition
Of permanent glass and transient flesh;

A visual reminder
Of our own mortality -
Not just some meat
That butchers had torn -
As a fountain pen filled
Out a cheque that was more
Than the cost of the Bentleys outside
In the evening-grey street;
Where the homeless were huddled
And an artist was seen,
With an ear to ear smile
Like the grin of a skull.

CHATTERTON

The ancestral muse is dead.
Its blood and ink coagulated
In a well of genius
That left no lines on suicide
Or any cryptic doggerel
That men could make inscriptions of.

All it left lay with it there;
Dead at the top of the winding stair
Where lover's footsteps never spiralled
Upwards to that dreary attic,
To remark upon the roof-top view
And conceive among the sonnets strewn

Like lilies for Ophelia,
With senses dragged by water weeds
To strange siestas of the dead,
In hedgerow shade eternities,
And flowers from the sunlight-dappled
Lanes that farthest childhood saw

With eyes that soaked the land, the sky,
Like sponges for a sullen craft
That veered between a gift and curse
Until its fragile shell imploded;
Holed and sunk like a galleon
In seas of cold indifference;
And left a word-confettied corpse
Lamented only by the sun
In shards of stained-glass window colour.

HOLLYWOOD

From a fourth floor window, Sunset Strip
Is sequined like a show girl's dress
That movie moguls once caressed
Before the fast-food outlets came
And riots scratched the thin veneer
Of glamour that had hid decay.

Twilight turns the smog-brown sky
A colour deep as mussel shells,
And silhouettes the ragged palms
To afro hair-dos crowned by stars
Beside a sun-baked asphalt snake
That lies in wait for unsuspecting
Tourists that have lost their way.

Backdrop hills take sinister shapes,
Like dark B-movie monsters lurking
In a lampless no-man's-land
Of affluence and effluent
Where pushers, pimps and pissed-on pavements
Pearl their tombstone smiles at passing
Wealth in lacquered limousines -
Like leeches on the AIDS infected
Wet-back whores and failed starlets;
Girls with a dollar lip-gloss smeared
Across the inert grin of chaos.

RADIO FOOTBALL

Each pass is met
By poor reception;
French pop radio
Interfering
With the play
And wingers weaving
In and out
Of frequency.
I cannot see
The free kick taken
Through a wall
Of names:
Some recognised -
Must be my team
On the attack,
"It's there!" The shout
Goes up. Who scored?
(Phone rings, door slams)
- Hard to tell. I think
It's ours, but
What's this now:
An opera singer
On the pitch?
She thinks it's all over,
(Batteries run out)
- It is.

SUNDAY EVENING

The world has washed its hands of us.
Left this village to whatever
Fate is lurking in the hedgerows -
Darker, now the galleon sun
Is slowly sinking - all hands lost
In slumber as her seeping cargo
Sets the patchwork fields alight;
While here we wait for death to end
These Sunday afternoons we spend
In slow clock ticking living rooms
Of threadbare chairs and buttered scones,
Like rabbits caught in burning stubble -
We are locked to land and sky,
In quiet acceptance of our fate;
The hour slowly slips away
Unnoticed with the Evensong
Of steeple bells, as dusk-drawn shade
Makes poplars take on unfamiliar
Silhouettes, like tall cloaked strangers
Closing in with cudgel night
Concealed beneath their cloud-dark capes.
But soon this wretched day will cease
Its sad still-life soliloquy
Of tree-top crows in harsh lament
For this, our doomed and dying planet.

VENICE STILL-LIFE

They brought ashore the silver dead
In rituals practised over centuries.
Washed and weighed and laid them out
Like open drawers of knives beside
The ink-exuding cuttlefish
In spineless tubs of tentacles
And baskets heaving with crustaceans;
Still alive as sun consumed
A mist intense with faceless spectres
From the sea-spawned generations
Who had hauled these nets before.

I found the morning's catch for sale
In the gothic *Pescheria*;
Where the still-life corpses spill
From scales of commerce into focus.
Fodder for my camera's eye
That moves with feline stealth among
Their stupid numbers; open mouthed
And gulping down the prow-disturbed
Reflections of indecent hours;
On their way to gutless ençores
As the local speciality.

ALICE

Alice wore my thirteenth Summer
Like a hedgerow-gathered garland;
Gleaned from meadows where my head
Lay cradled in her gingham lap.

Beside the river's shrunken vein,
Our minds and tadpole jars lay empty;
Watching aimless cabbage-whites
Disturb the still with stuttered flight.

Each waking hour I sought that maiden,
Like some swarthy village suitor;
Under churchyard yew tree shade
Words were brought like floral tokens
To her flowing, flaxen altar.

But our pacts of love turned cold
As stars and twilight swallows cut
The insect air with dusky rituals;
Screeching at me from the eaves
To come back through the looking glass.

LAS VEGAS

She sits like a jewel in the tanned expanse
Of a belly dancer's navel swelter.
A city from nothing - almost as if
A neon-erupting spaceship had landed
And sent out a crew shaped like Joshua trees
To roam its stark perimeter
Forever in the steel-hard sun.

The shimmer of the day gives way
To night, and brake-light tracer bullets
From the cars in downtown flight;
Like neurones sending impulses
Of sin across the tattooed dark,
Where mobster sewn illuminations
Make the sky-bound stars seem dull
In contrast to their cabaret.

Losers beg elusive riches
From the green baize deities,
But all they find is artificial
Temples, tarts and neon spilling
Out from every orifice
That serves a honey-seeking swarm
With 24 hour, all-you-can-eat
Extravaganzas of excess;
With *ring-and-flowers-thrown-in* chapels
Using cattle principles
To marry flame haired carnivores
To old men on conveyor belts.

What you see is what you get;
A cardboard cut-out movie set
Of hotels using semi-naked
Girls as male tractor beams,
In plastic, themed environments
Designed to make the act of stealing
Seem like harmless entertainment.

DIARY OF A TWELVE YEAR OLD GIRL

Eggs are scarce as smiles round here,
So breakfast is some feta cheese
Left over from the last food parcel.

Mornings *always* start like this -
A lull before the muffled drum
Of counter-offensive shelling scatters
Starlings from apartment eaves
Like feathered shrapnel in the sun,
And bursts of stray machine-gun fire
Cackle like some mechanical witch.

Your days are half-dark sentences
Of rooms tattooed by pins of light
That sneak through every chink of shutter
Like an angel seeking refuge
From the indiscriminate guns
Of snipers shooting *anyone*
They catch in telescopic sights.

Then, sometimes, when the killing stops
Your Father makes you read aloud
From books that are your education
Now that schools are burned-out shells
Or makeshift military hospitals;
And squeezes smiles like used-up toothpaste
When he draws the pencil marks
That show how tall you're getting now
Your thirteenth birthday is approaching -
Saying "soon it will be over."
Then you'll get the biggest ice cream
Ever seen in Sarajevo.

SUBURBAN BLUES

I *tried* to teach myself the blues
But found my fingers far too white
To know the usual inspiration
Of ancestral slavery,
Or Summers spent on misery's porch
Composing three-chord requiems
For whisky, women; all things
That don't reside in Bromley, Kent.

But I practised all the same;
Sat in my suburban bedroom
Stretching strings and imitating
BB King's distinctive growl
With songs about despair and leaving
Town on Highway sixty-one,
With sorrow in a battered suitcase
And the Mississippi sun's face pressed
Against my bug-smeared windshield view
Of diners at deserted junctions,
Freight trains crossing empty streets
And bars where you can get a shot
Of bourbon with your last two dollars.

In the end I got quite good;
But somehow it is not convincing
When an upwardly mobile man
Attempts to murmur Deep-South blues.

KITE

The sky was scoured white that Winter.
Bleached beyond the wind-whipped trees
That found me tousled, like a Hawthorn
Perched up on this chalky ridge,
With grass worn thin by a thousand years
Of ruminants and men.

Below me thrust the village steeple
Catching sun on oxide sails
That locked the land to dubious heaven;
Where my kite, in red and yellow
Jester's garb, had climbed beyond
My calling like some cloth-eared Icarus.

High above the fresh-ploughed fields,
With insolence, conveyed through trembling
String, my kite ran rings around
A tractor scratching flint cursed earth
Like furrows on a worried brow.

Its wake was filled with screaming gulls,
In carnival or death procession.
Whiter than the chalk exposed,
And sheep, in distant hillside huddle.

THE SKELETON AT THE FEAST

Though poverty had been unkind,
They made the sparsely furnished room
A shrine of flowers and sugar skulls,
In celebration of the dead
Who leave their graves in sun-baked earth
To dance with painted skeletons.

Today the widows will not weep
When candles light a sepia generation
Ageless, now their souls inhabit
Sun-drenched yellow afternoons,
Like shadows stretched in quiet cloisters
Where the lipless lovers whisper.

Twilight sends savannah darkness
Searching all the lampless land
For souls beyond a carnival
That milked the moonlit mausoleums
Of this town's ancestral ghosts,
And brought them singing to the feast.

COMMON FIRE

They say the fire had been ignited
By a passing onion seller's
Carelessly discarded Gaulloises:
Whoof! The dry brown bracken tinderbox
Of Iron Age barrows, silver birch
And camps with 'Keep Out' signs, went up
In flames that took three days to turn
The contours of our burial ground
(Where victims of the plague were laid
To rest) into a blackened waste
Of bare scorched gorse and skeleton trees;
The village elders stood and mused
With arms akimbo: "Never seen
A sight like this in fifty years" they said, as walls
Of smoke eclipsed the sun and beat
The firemen from three counties back
With heat and change in wind direction.
Us, whose secret hideouts were
Destroyed, were more indignant than
The women shaking soot from knickers
Hung on village washing lines;
And though we found some spent tank shells,
The cataclysm marked my childhood
Far beyond that stifled Summer.

KEEPSAKE

Remember me, like Eros, plunging
Arrows in your circus heart
Or swooning over roses set
Adrift upon your skin's white ocean.

Think of me when iron railing
Shadows stretch like gold-leaved zebras,
Loose among the stone-faced mews
Of Pimlico, on silent hooves.

Remember me now stars caress
Your face in silver shoals that catch
The moon, then burn a few brief moments
On your dream's relentless tide.

Think of me beside you now;
As close as stained-glass petals strewn
Across your skin in vivid colours
Like Matisse's death-bed snail.

ROCKS

We got them from the railway line
As crickets rubbed their violin legs,
And adders lay absorbing sun
Among the bracken heads that curled
Like tops of bishops' crosiers.

The stones that made our pockets bulge
Were granite - flecked like speckled eggs,
From intervals between the black
Remains of decomposing sleepers
Ripped up on the disused track.

And after moss had been washed off,
We took them to the factory;
Where someone had each rock encased
In plastic, with a guarantee
Of xeroxed authenticity
That it was from the slopes of Everest,
Or the surface of the Moon.

I did not see it as illegal;
Just promotion from the ranks
For rocks that once were ordinary.

WET WEEKEND

We are not here to watch the rain
Caress some closed-up hot dog stands,
And street lamps flaking salt-peeled paint
Along the shiny promenade,
With strings of opaque fairy lights
That hang unpicked like ghostly pears
Or snuffed-out stars that need replacing.

Besides, the view is irrelevant,
If nineteen-sixties psychedelic
Curtains cover guest house windows,
So our only sense of seaside
Is a barely audible hiss
Of shingle on receding foam
And seagulls crying on the wind
Like children for a stick of rock

We are not here for anything,
Except a wet weekend of sex.

TATTOO

The tattooed rose upon your breast
Seemed out of place -
It did not fit
My first impression of you, sat
Like one of Renoir's sun-soaked subjects,
Sipping chocolate-dusted cups
Of cappuccino, as I played
Dessert spoon surgeon with your past;
Uncovering that last, dark secret,
With the aid of Frank Sinatra -
Crooning over tiramasu,
Until you let my fingers trace
Those petals, spilling breathless colour
Over moon-white flesh, like fire.